Life Sights ™
INSIGHTS
INTO THE
INDIVIDUAL
CHRISTIAN LIFE

Book Two

Old Self/New Self

T. George Homsher,
M.Ed. Counseling Psychology

Acknowledgments

*To God the Father, God the Son and God the Holy Spirit
for our wonderful loving relationship.*

*To Howard Blandau for the true Christian love he gave me.
I am grateful for our father-son relationship.*

*To my dear wife, Denise for our incredible love
and marriage all these years.*

*To my dear daughter Bethany, I am appreciative of our
special loving relationship; especially as a Home School
dad and house-husband during the critical years of her
childhood. They have been the best years of my life.*

*To my Mom whom I love, who taught me an
important element of character when I was growing up:
"Georgie, no halfway!"*

*Finally, a book of quality must have experts to provide
the high-quality "finishing touches."
With this in mind, I sincerely thank Melissa Hardin
for her outstanding editing, and Victoria Robinette Merkel
for her top-shelf book design and composition work.*

Contents

T. George Homsher
LifeSights: Book Two- Old Self / New Self
Copyright © 2011 T. George Homsher
All rights reserved
ISBN 978-0-9829736-1-5

Book Cover and Composition by Robinette Creative Services
Book Editing by Melissa Hardin
Published by Unto Jesus Not Men, LLC
www.untojesusnotmen.com

Introduction

Old Self/New Self

This book encourages greater understanding in living in the new self. The new self is an incredible reality for our Christian lives, for we have truly been born again. It is in the new self that we can live a victorious Christian life and allow the Lord Jesus Christ to become our life. When we live in the new self, we are helping and not hurting, bringing peace not fear, and giving joy not misery. With the breakdown of our society and the end times that are upon us, the old self is rearing its ugly existence. Many good Christians are being broadsided by non-Christians and by Christians who are living with the old self. It seems more and more people living in the worst elements of the old self are making it very difficult for those who are not.

This book seeks to help Christians discern who is living in the old self and who is living in the new self. Many people living in the old self mask their intentions, which makes it easier for them to carry out their deeds. This is why distinguishing the opposing behaviors is necessary, as is the awareness of the enormous amounts of hurt, fear and misery that someone living in the old self can create.

Chapter 1

The Old Self in America

Renowned psychologist Howard Blandau describes the deterioration of America as a distinct change in individual character. Human character can be presented as man's attempt to develop the best of a new self with a non-spiritual approach. In this regard, character can be defined as traits that are derived from morality, principles and the implementation of the best of what a human being can be. These traits would include courage, forthrightness, honesty, endurance, stability, being positive, consistency of mind, reliability and many others. Blandau believed that prior to the 1960s, about 75% of the American population had, what he considered to be, good character. The remaining 25% had little or poor character. In the early to mid-1990s, he believed those percentages flipped, resulting in only 25% of Americans having good character. Blandau's evaluation is a catastrophic turnaround in regard to the integrity and character of our nation that is made up of individuals.

Before the 1960s when America had an abundance of character in its society, the non-Christian could more readily imitate those around them. We tend to become like those around us (for better or worse), so if a non-Christian living in the old self surrounded himself with people living in the new self, he would be positively influenced and able to develop a strong character. However, the ability for the non-Christian to develop a character in current American culture is difficult, simply because of the prevalence of those who lack character.

People who do not have character do not identify with or respect the character in others. Before the 1960s, individuals who lacked character was outnumbered three to one and their lack of respect for those who did have character was in the minority. They were seen as negative, and many chose to develop character because they were outnumbered.

In recent times, individuals without character have seized the upper hand and are using their lack of respect to a very negative advantage. This disrespect is also fueled by those who are secularists, and seek a non-Christian America. The irony is that non-Christians have taken an enormous hit when it comes to feeling good about themselves. They have embraced the old self (character-lacking self), and all of its tragedy. They have left the high decency of the character-filled life, and are no longer identifying with it.

BEGINNING OF THE SHIFT

In 1948, Blandau accepted a position as a chaplain at an Iowa boys' reformatory. He was in his 20s and had left his hometown in the Philadelphia, Pennsylvania area, unsure of his ability to help 350 difficult boys. During the next seven years, he led many hardened, troubled boys to a saving faith in the Lord Jesus Christ. These were young men who were living the old self lifestyle and getting into all kinds of trouble. Many of them had lost hope, and as a consequence had found a negative direction in life. Ultimately, many of the boys saw something new and different in the Chaplain, turned away from their old ways and began to live new lives in Jesus Christ.

At the end of seven years at the reformatory, Blandau took a job in a Christian college and began to see a troubling pattern. The Christian girls and boys were no different than the reformatory boys when it came to character. He expelled many students for immoral behavior. He found the difference between the reformatory boys and the college students was that the boys in the reformatory were breaking the law with out-in-the-open delinquency and then were punished. The Christians were living in an immoral, secretive non-Christian lifestyle, and were not getting caught.

Both the delinquent boys and the college students were reacting to the anxieties and hurts of their background in different ways. The boys in the reformatory were not stuffing their emotions inside, but were being very impulsive and letting them out regardless of the consequences. The Christian students were keeping their hurt, anger, and anxiety of emotions inside. Those emotions built up and caused stomach trouble, headaches and other physical ailments, along with compulsiveness toward immorality.

Many of the Christian students were head-high in old self living. This is why, as we will discuss later, many non-Christians do not see much of a difference between Christians and non-Christians. Many are in a pattern like these students who were not living in the new self, and were not able to face their emotional turmoil.

Paving the Way for the Old Self: The Secularization of America

There were many factors that fueled the old self lifestyle in America. Secularization (non-religion) of once-Christian America included a focus on things that were not religious, as well as an adversarial role directly against Christians. This attack employed old self tactics such as shame and embarrassment in embracing faith. Many Christians were swept into this tidal surge and became embarrassed by their own faith and of the Lord Jesus Christ. Many individual Christians became afraid of declaring their faith in an open manner where this was commonplace in our country for countless years. Countless Christians began to live in the old self without realizing what was happening. A negative pattern of this sort is extremely difficult to break, especially if someone is not aware he is in it or how it is negatively affecting him.

Other secular initiatives, including abortion, taking God out of the public school system, and the sewage on television and the Internet, are the result of the initial assault described above when Christians stood down when it was time to stand up for their faith. To combat these initiatives, Christians must declare the name of Jesus without reservation. There is much power in declaring the name of Jesus and taking a stand for Him openly and without shame. This is a simple yet dynamic way to turn the tide of the secular assault on our Christian faith, because secularists hate the name of Jesus, and they hate when we speak it.

PAVING THE WAY FOR THE OLD SELF: THE SECULARIZATION OF CHRISTIAN CHURCHES IN AMERICA

Not only was religion taken out of many areas of public life in America, but also out of many churches. Many churches resemble country clubs, instead of places of worship of the Father, places of focus on the Son and places of dependency on the Spirit. Many leaders and attendees have lost their focus on the Lord Jesus Christ as the center of their Christian faith.

The most powerful problem in evangelical Christianity is a focus on principles instead of a relationship with the Godhead. In this context, the term "principles" refers to proper beliefs, discipline, rights and wrongs, commandments and many other elements of living morally and with integrity. The problem with emphasizing principles over relationship is that principles don't necessarily lead to a relationship with the Godhead. However, a relationship with God the Father, God the Son and God the Holy Spirit will automatically bring about the right principles. In his book, *He That is Spiritual*, Dr. Lewis Sperry Chafer, shows that a dependence on the Holy Spirit dynamically reveals and glorifies Christ to us (John 16:12–15) as our focal point and closest relationship in our Christian faith. From this exaltation of Jesus by the Holy Spirit we find ourselves in a much more intimate relationship with Him. When we have this, then we are able to have a measure of fellowship and access with God the Father (Ephesians 2:18), and be able to truly glory, honor and praise Him (John 14:6–7 says, *"Jesus saith unto him, I am the way, the truth, and the life: no man cometh unto the Father, but by me. If ye had known me, ye should have known my Father also: and from henceforth ye know him, and have seen him."*)

Many churches have decided to emphasize the principles of rights and wrongs of the Christian faith as a major focal point of their teaching. This comes from an overwhelming majority of church leaders who are pragmatic, practical and organizational. They function well in the structure of most American churches, which are institutionalized and are part of larger organizations. The practical individual would feel much more comfortable discussing the rights and wrongs rather than discussing relationships with the Godhead. This is why a balance in church leadership with the inclusion of more insightful, discerning and social personalities is key. Social Christians will discern a proper balance of pragmatics and relationships with the Godhead.

With the emphasis on the principles of right and wrong, many churches have become involved with accountability partners or groups. This "accountability movement" emerged as a practical solution to encourage individuals to do the right thing, which ultimately led to emphasizing the relationships to their life partners instead of with the Lord Jesus. Many times a partner who is keeping the other accountable has problems of his own. This is a double axe of negativity, and the focus becomes the problems and not on the solutions. The accountability approach came out of the group therapy movement, which fosters dependency on individuals or on the group itself. That is why it is surprising to see so many conservative Christians becoming involved in this kind of approach. The true conservative approach to Christianity places great emphasis on the strengthening of the individual and not a dependency on others. The Bible discusses our accountability in major form as being to God the Father (Romans 14:12) and the Lord Jesus where the Apostle Peter says in 1 Peter 4:5, "*Who shall give account to him that is ready to judge the quick and the dead."* This gives us an urgency to develop that wonderful close relationship with Jesus to make sure that we are unto Him and not to people.

Many churches need to return to an emphasis on the discipleship of individual Christians. When a person is in discipleship with Jesus, he develops intimacy with Him, instead of with the person holding him accountable. Discipleship in Jesus imitates the process that He was involved with Himself.

An over-emphasis on teaching (many times not on Jesus), and less of an emphasis on worship erodes our sense of discipleship. When we sing to the Father and to Jesus, it brings our focus back to why we are at church in the first place. Over time, many Christians have found it difficult to completely focus on the Lord Jesus.

With many churches losing their focus on Jesus, there has been a staggering number of new self Christians leaving the institutionalized church and going to the home church. What is left in many churches are old self Christians who do not take their faith and their relationship with the Lord Jesus seriously. Church leaders often do not deal with these old self Christians in a timely fashion (First Corinthians 5:9–13), which often leads to an exodus of new self Christians. Old self Christians or old self non-Christians who have made their way into the church are creating a problem that needs to be dealt with in Christian love and forgiveness. Many church leaders are not aware of the havoc these individuals can create until it's much too late.

Chapter 2

The Grim Reality of
the Old Self

In our mother's womb, we are conceived into the old self. The King James version of the Bible calls it the "old man," but we will use the term "old self," because it's easier to understand and refers to each and every individual. The old self reminds us we are terribly lost and in need of a Savior. There is great potential for an enormous amount of evil (Romans 7:18–19). A review of history books shows evil has almost always overwhelmed the good and that there have been many more old self individuals than new self individuals (John 3:19). For as long as we are in the human flesh we will always have to contend with the old self and its incredible power, evil and overwhelming propensity for self-destruction.

No one will be perfect until we are face to face with the Lord Jesus in Paradise, so we always need and long for our Savior. Jesus has enabled us to be born again and possess a new self. This does not prevent us from difficulty and tragedy in our lives. However Jesus not only saved us initially for eternal salvation, but for every day of our born-again lives.

A MATTER OF DEATH OR LIFE

God wills us to work out our salvation so that we can prove to be His good soldiers (Second Timothy 2:3). Life is not an easy ride; many times it is a very painful and difficult one (First Peter 4:12–13). Working out our salvation is often the old self versus the new self. It is literally an inner struggle of two opposing forces. This does not mean that we engage in an internal battle - that kind of a battle was won by the Lord Jesus who conquered all things, even death. However it does mean that we need to die to this old self, and put on the new self's life (Romans 6:6–11; Galatians 5:24). There are many Christians who focus on death and not on life. This is a major issue that determines whether one is going to get beyond the old self to the new self. When we focus on the old self, we take our eyes off the new life that the Godhead is offering. We wallow in the old self; full of guilt and hopelessness, instead of embracing the new life full of freedom, joy, love, hope, peace and so many other incredible things.

The Bible says that we (the old selves) were crucified with Christ when we became believers (Galatians 2:20). This is our identification of our union with Jesus' death and crucifixion with our old self. When He died, our old selves died, but even after we are saved, we still have to reconcile and move past the old self. The old self still has a lot of substance and the ability to destroy us. What emerges is the need for the continual process of dying to the old self (First Corinthians 15:31). It is a process that continues until the day we die. We need not be preoccupied by this ongoing heightened negativity and struggle, for we have One who will deal with this battle while we focus on journey to the new self.

The Apostle Paul presents this struggle where he describes the situation of the old self as dead, and the emergence of the new life in Jesus. Jesus has brought us life and has conquered death. *"I protest by your rejoicing which I have in Christ Jesus our Lord, I die daily."* (First Corinthians 15:31) In Romans 6:6–11, he goes on to say, *"Knowing this, that our old man is crucified with him, that the body of sin might be destroyed, that henceforth we should not serve sin. For he that is dead is freed from sin. Now if we be dead with Christ, we believe that we shall also live with him: Knowing that Christ being raised from the dead dieth no more; death hath no more dominion over him. For in that he died, he died unto sin once: but in that he liveth, he liveth unto God. Likewise reckon ye also yourselves to be dead indeed unto sin, but alive unto God through Jesus Christ our Lord."*

Paul dynamically continues our theme of death and life in Galatians 2:20, but focuses on a preoccupation on life: *"I am crucified with Christ: Nevertheless I live; yet not I, but Christ liveth in me: and the life which I now live in the flesh I live by the faith of the Son of God, who loved me, and gave himself for me."*

What Paul is saying is that our identification is on the old self crucified with Jesus. We have a new life that is literally in Jesus. Our new self life that is still in the fallen, sinful flesh is to be lived out in faith through love (Galatians 5:5–6). The focus is not on the negative of death, but on the incredible new life coming from a loving, sacrificial God. We are beyond the old self death, if we focus on the new life we have in a loving relationship with the Godhead. When we focus on the old self it takes the place of the new self we now have as born-again Christians.

It is however important to understand that there is plenty of hope for Christians who are living in the new self, but there is not plenty of hope for Christians and non-Christians who are living in the old self. Paul demonstrates this clearly as he opens up the enormous problem that we still have: (Ephesians 4:22–32) *"That ye put off concerning the former conversation the old man, which is corrupt according to the deceitful lusts; And be renewed in the spirit of your mind; And that ye put on the new man, which after God is created in righteousness and true holiness. Wherefore putting away lying, speak every man truth with his neighbour: for we are members one of another. Be ye angry, and sin not: let not the sun go down upon your wrath: Neither give place to the devil Let him that stole steal no more: but rather let him labour, working with his hands the thing which is good, that he may have to give to him that needeth. Let no corrupt communication proceed out of your mouth, but that which is good to the use of edifying, that it may minister grace unto the hearers. And grieve not the holy Spirit of God, whereby ye are sealed unto the day of redemption. Let all bitterness, and wrath, and anger, and clamour, and evil speaking, be put away from you, with all malice: And be ye kind one to another, tenderhearted, forgiving one another, even as God for Christ's sake hath forgiven you."*

Underlying Characteristics of the Old Self

- Control is perhaps the most dynamic of all the underlying characteristics of the old self. This type of control is a form of domination, or a level of authoritarianism. This would not be referring to character-filled leadership, but in situations of taking away others' freedom. The most important insight regarding the issue of control in a person's life is the more control (not self-control) one seeks, the more evil. Less control means less evil. The old self individual who controls at this level often can't help himself, because this behavior is a way of avoiding insecurity and weakness.

This type of individual has developed a dynamic feedback in controlling others. The energy and pleasure from this behavior encourages this individual to put others in the bondage of control; to use others in any way he wants. The old self individual is very selfish and there is little or no concept of loving or giving to others.

- These individuals are very adept at using emotions and communication. They will falsely present themselves, falsely accuse others, cheat, lie and may perform many other manipulating behaviors to get their way. Manipulation is the major vehicle to control and use others. They are so good at using emotion for their own purposes, they do not know how to comfortably rejoice with those who rejoice or weep with those who weep (Romans 12:15). They do not know how to empathize with others, apologize or seek forgiveness.

- The old self lifestyle is one of sin, and one who bears that lifestyle bears the burden of guilt. Living in a pattern of the old self is contrary to God's will. This doesn't mean a Christian is going to be perfect. It does mean the individual should avoid patterns of sin that help define old self living. Many Christians are trying to live with the old self and the new self. They may attend church, read the Bible, listen to Christian music or do many other things that may seem appropriate for a Christian life. However, when these things are done while living an old self life, the positive Christian things are nullified. It not only nullifies those things, but it creates enormous guilt for trying to live both lives in one. There are many Christians who go on psychopharmacological medication because of the anxiety of the double life they are living. Rather than face the sin in their lives and cease the old self pattern, many Christians continue on to even more emotional and psychological trauma.

DEALING WITH OLD SELF INDIVIDUALS

Ephesians 4:14–15 *"That we henceforth be no more children, tossed to and fro, and carried about with every wind of doctrine, by the sleight of men, and cunning craftiness, whereby they lie in wait to deceive; But speaking the truth in love, may grow up into him in all things, which is the head, even Christ:"*

Although there are some old self individuals who are living openly and unashamedly in this way of life, many times we do not readily recognize it. They do this in an incredibly manipulative, calculating and aloof way. Many times by the time we recognize we have been dealing with this kind of individual, we have already felt intense hurt and anxiety. As the Apostle Paul proclaims, they create a serious form of confusion by confusing our mind ("every wind of doctrine"), slighting or hurting us, or using clever and dirty tricks ("cunning craftiness"). It is often shocking when a new self Christian experiences these deceptions from an old self Christian.

When we realize where old self individuals are coming from, new self individuals should be upfront and speak the truth in love as the Lord Jesus or the Apostle Paul would have done. It is best to live life in this forthright manner. Sometimes this upfront approach may need to be done with a tender heart or with a firm approach. The Lord Jesus and Paul had spoken to old self individuals using different approaches. Paul demonstrates this where he says to the Corinthians *"What will ye? Shall I come unto you with a rod, or in love, and in the spirit of meekness?"* (First Corinthians 4:21)

The necessary approach is up to God the Father. One always needs to do His approach rather than one's own. When one is upfront and speaking the truth in love it helps to put the old self individual and what they are doing out in the open where they are much more uncomfortable. Initially, especially with old self Christians, they may become very defensive and quite negative. However, because things are out in the open they may eventually respect the new insights.

Take the case of Steve who took the risk to open up to his friend Bill. Although both had attended different churches they become close friends. However, when Bill lost his job he became highly negative. For many weeks he simmered with resentment, and at times was shockingly malicious. Steve tried to put it off as the loss of a job and the difficulties surrounding that. Yet, he couldn't help but notice his own resentment of the way Bill had treated him and many others. Usually when a person is making one person miserable, they are often making many others miserable. In fact, Steve saw how Bill was treating his family and other friends. He felt a responsibility for himself and his own negativity he was experiencing from Bill, but he also felt a responsibility to the others in Bill's life who were also suffering. He needed to be forthright with Bill about his behavior. He also realized he had to speak his mind because, through his own resentment, he was becoming like Bill. Steve phoned Bill, took a deep breath, and went to his house for a meeting. Sometimes it is best to send a letter (it all depends on the relationship), but in this case, Steve felt he needed to discuss the matter in person.

Steve prayed the whole way to Bill's house. He was unsure how it would turn out, so he simply asked the Lord Jesus. Jesus told Steve to prepare for a difficult talk but a hopeful future for their relationship. Of course, this made Steve feel even more anxious so he asked the Lord Jesus for peace, strength and wisdom during the meeting.

Bill opened their talk with a joke. "So, what's all this meeting of the minds we are going to do? I'd rather us being mindless and playing pool downstairs instead."

Steve responded, "Well, Bill actually what I wanted to talk to you about is rather serious."

At that, Bill became much more serious, which added to Steve's fear. He quickly prayed to the Lord Jesus to give him peace as he began speaking, "The reason I wanted to set up this meeting is because I was very concerned with how you are doing with losing your job, and the difficulty that must have brought you emotionally. I want to be honest – I'm feeling resentful about the way you've negatively treated me lately. I don't think it's Christian to be resentful, and I certainly don't want to put that on you, but I think it's already leaking out and I apologize."

Bill quickly reacted to what Steve was saying. "What are you talking about? I'm not sure this is the kind of discussion friends have with each other."

Immediately, Steve sensed Bill's defensiveness. He ended their short meeting by letting Bill know he felt they needed to discuss this matter more, but that he certainly respected Bill's desire not to discuss it at that time. Steve said he enjoyed their friendship and he would be available when Bill was ready to talk.

Bill understandably was confused, and closed the meeting with an attitude of negativity.

As the weeks progressed Bill began to reflect and pray about what happened with Steve. His initial anger began to give way to openness and he started honestly looking at his behavior. He kept coming back to the reality that his choices weren't good at all. He also thought of this great friendship with Steve, and how he didn't want it to be distant. Bill knew that Steve was a wonderful Christian man who took a risk as a Christian and had opened up to him. After speaking with his wife, Bill decided to set up a meeting with Steve. Bill let Steve know how much his unemployment was hurting and scaring him. Bill apologized for his bad behavior, and said he did not want any resentfulness to get in the way of their friendship.

It is possible for a person living in the old self to get beyond that lifestyle, but sometimes this is not the case. Sometimes a relationship ends when the person living in the old self becomes offended by the forthright nature of a friend or family member. If this happens, there are some important things to remember. The first is that you can't do any more than you can do. This may sound flippant, but in reality it comes down to this simple phrase. Many times we can only take a person or a friendship so far. If we've been forthright with a person and they take that negatively or angrily, they will have to live in the heartache or misery of it all. We deal with them the best we can and then we move on. Life is too short to carry the burdens of others when they are unwilling to face and take ownership of their choices. It is our responsibility to let them be at this point, and focus on controlling your own behavior and not theirs.

Chapter 3

Some Tricks of the
Old Self Trade

FALSE ACCUSATIONS

A brutal tactic of old self individuals is the weapon of false accusation, which has its origins in resentment or bitterness. As Christians we need not be shocked when false accusations occur because the Lord Jesus endured many. In Luke 11:53–54 it says, *"And as he said these things unto them, the scribes and the Pharisees began to urge him to vehemently, and to provoke him to speak of many things: laying wait for him, and seeking to watch something out of his mouth, that they may accuse him."*

False accusations can escalate into malice and unrighteous wrath where the old self individual seeks to exact punishment on someone else, even if that someone else is innocent.

New Unger's Bible Dictionary defines malice in this way, "MALICE (Gk. kakia, "badness," 1 Cor. 5:8; Ephes. 4:31; Col. 3:8; Titus 3:3; 1

Peter 2:1). This Gk. word denotes a vicious disposition, evilness, or wickedness. A kindred word is in Romans 1:29 (Gk. kakoetheia, "bad character"), given by Paul in his long list of Gentile sins and implying malignant subtlety or malicious craftiness. Aristotle defines malice as "taking all things in the evil part" (Rhetoric 2.13), as the Geneva version of the Scriptures likewise renders it. It is "that peculiar form of evil which manifests itself in a malignant interpretation of the actions of others, an attributing of them all to the worst motive" (Trench, Synonyms of the NT, p. 11)."

Many times those who falsely accuse do so when they know they will not face accusatory reciprocity. This seems to be mimicking what is going on in our hostile political, legal and religious environments. This is a similar arena with similar types of individuals that Jesus had to contend with - the Sadducees (more political than religious types), the lawyers (highly calculating types) and the Pharisees (religious types).

Many times false accusers will accuse someone else of doing something that they themselves are doing. It is an attempt to put their guilt onto someone else so they can soften their own guilt (Romans 2:21–22). They will also do this to cover the scent on their path so their deception will not be discovered. As the false accusations become more intense, the false accuser covers up an enormous amount of sin and evil that they may eventually unload punishingly onto someone else.

There are key things a Christian needs to do to overcome this difficult situation:

If an individual feels innocent of an accusation, he needs to avoid accepting any serious guilt in the matter. If one is unsure, he should allow God to do the searching if there is any guilt to be owned (Philippians 3:15). If our heart does not condemn us than we shouldn't feel guilty or condemn ourselves (Romans 14:22; First John 3:21). If one accepts false guilt in this situation he will have a real sense of condemnation in spirit, often feel fearful (or anxious), and ultimately play right into the hands of the false accuser. It also plays right into the hands of Satan who will pile even more guilt onto the innocent Christian. The truth sets us free, so it is vital to take ownership of innocence and of the truth in our mind and in our heart. This will allow the individual to redirect his mind and heart from this highly negative situation and more quickly move on from it.

If the accusations are severe, it is best to cease any relationship with the false accuser (First Corinthians 5:9–13). God the Father normally does not want us to continue on with this kind of vindictive person, especially if the accusations stem from malice or unrighteous wrath. These relationships typically end because the severe false accusations that one levels against another often leave little or no room for reparation. Whether communicated directly with the person who is falsely accusing or is simply experienced inwardly, the mindset with a false accuser usually needs to be "Goodbye forever."

It is also important to not see something that ends as a failure. Many times when situations or relationships end, we are given the chance to make decisions that will help us develop more character and possibly provide better opportunities. When we bear the sense of failure within ourselves that gives us a terrible sense of insecurity and confusion. Giving the burden to Jesus helps us make the most of every new situation.

A person who falsely accuses is aggressively rejecting a relationship. This kind of situation can cause us a great deal of hurt and fear. However, if the Christian withdraws their relationship with the accuser, the rejection becomes a two-way street. This may provide the new self Christian a sense of strength and the freedom from carrying bags of rejection from the old self individual.

The Bible says that Jesus has all judgment now, in John 5:22 it says, *"For the Father judgeth no man, but hath committed all judgment unto the Son."* Therefore, His vengeance instead of our vengeance is good enough for our lives. We as Christians are called to always forgive those who sin against us, and avoid any sense, much less action of, revenge or hatred on others. This approach to looking at Jesus and His judgment, however, can still be a minor emphasis of help in dealing with those who falsely accuse us.

We can be confident that those who come against us open themselves up to the corrections of the Lord Jesus (Second Timothy 4:14; 2 Peter 2:16; Galatians 5:10). Psalms 3:4–8 says, *"I cried unto the LORD with my voice, and he heard me out of his holy hill. Selah. I laid me down and slept; I awaked; for the LORD sustained me. I will not be afraid of ten thousands of people, that have set themselves against me round about. Arise, O LORD;*

save me, O my God: for thou hast smitten all mine enemies upon the cheek bone; thou hast broken the teeth of the ungodly. Salvation belongeth unto the LORD: thy blessing is upon thy people. Selah."

The false accuser and Satan would like us to take ownership of their flaming missile guilt, but remembering that Jesus will judge the guilty can reinforce our innocence. This is not to be done in glee or self-satisfaction, but in championing our Savior Jesus and His appropriate work to protect us and deal with sin against us (First Peter 3:12). False accusers don't know they will be judged by Jesus. To the degree of the false accusation Jesus will judge them to that level or beyond (First Peter 3:16; Second Peter 2:1–6; Second Timothy 3:9 and 4:14–15; Galatians 5:10).

A very powerful approach to dealing with a false accuser is to assess his background, and how it has influenced his life. If he had discussed a lot of difficult or negative situations it is reasonable to assume there are more unspoken issues. People who have not dealt with pain and difficulty in their past are controlled by negative emotions that resonate into the present. If we can see the impact of a troubled past, it will help us to not take this situation quite so personally, even if the false accusations are very painful. We can be more open to still loving that person, even if we have moved on from the relationship. Our love can go a long way in moving past this painful situation, and the love for the Godhead bodily will be more immediately felt even in the midst of this difficulty.

Destroyers of Relationships

Old self individuals have a strong tendency to destroy relationships with debate and division. The Strong's Talking Greek & Hebrew Dictionary defines debate and division:

> "Debate- of uncertain affinity; a *quarrel*, i.e. (by implication) *wrangling* :- contention, debate, strife, variance."

> "Division- from (schizo); a split or gap (*"schism"*), literal or figurative: division, rent, schism."

It is simply the old saying: "Divide and conquer." They may be jealous of other people's relationships or successes. They may just be tired of a current relationship. They use debating, division, criticism, gossip and other tools to destroy relationships. A red flag appears when someone is openly criticizing someone else behind his back without any desire for resolution. If they're criticizing someone in front of you, you can imagine what are they saying to someone else about you.

Sexual Perversion

For Christians predominance of sexual perversion is the external result of an internal issue. The overwhelming majority of sexual perversion comes from bottled-up emotions. A buildup of hurt, anxiety, loneliness or stress becomes increasingly intense and leads to compulsive, uncontrollable behavior. Compulsive sinful behavior is the result of not dealing with those emotions. This is not an excuse to sin, but to help stop sinning because if we know the origin of our problems, we can more likely solve them.

The vast percentage of sexually immoral behavior from non-Christian individuals comes from the flesh. Many unbelievers, like many Christians, have made sexuality the most dynamic and energizing part of their lives. That focus may be appealing because it creates a lot of internal energy. However, it is an immature lifestyle that becomes dependent on sex, and endures all of the subsequent negative consequences.

Chapter 4

The New Self

The new self is a new birth the moment someone becomes a Christian. Believing in the Lord Jesus saves us, but we are born again by the Holy Spirit. Paul talks about this in Titus 3:4–6 where he said, *"But after that the kindness and love of God our Saviour toward man appeared, Not by works of righteousness which we have done, but according to his mercy he saved us, by the washing of regeneration, and renewing of the Holy Ghost; Which he shed on us abundantly through Jesus Christ our Saviour;"*

As the Holy Spirit conceived the Lord Jesus in Mary (Luke 1:35) likewise He brings about our new birth (John 3:5). The difference is that the Lord Jesus was fully God but became fully physically man, whereas we are reborn not into a new physical body, but into a spiritual new self. This new life is in the spiritual realm, which is the most deep, dynamic and energizing area of our lives. Our body is called the temple of the Holy Spirit (First Corinthians 6:19), and while it is true in our flesh dwells no good thing, in our bodies dwells an enormous amount of good.

In John 3:3–8 Jesus said, *"Verily, verily, I say unto thee, Except a man be born again, he cannot see the kingdom of God. Nicodemus saith unto him, How can a man be born when he is old? Can he enter the second time into his mother's womb, and be born? Jesus answered, Verily, verily, I say unto thee, Except a man be born of water and of the Spirit, he cannot enter into the kingdom of God. That which is born of the flesh is flesh; and that which is born of the Spirit is spirit. Marvel not that I said unto thee, Ye must be born again. The wind bloweth where it listeth, and thou hearest the sound thereof, but canst not tell whence it cometh, and whither it goeth: so is every one that is born of the Spirit."*

Like Nicodemus a new self being born of water and Spirit perplexes many Christians. Perhaps that is because 75% of Americans are practical thinkers, which makes it more difficult to understand things that are not seen. The other 25% of individuals are creative; they use more imagination, see a multitude of colors and are more able to understand things unseen.

The Bible commentator Matthew Henry, in *Matthew Henry's Commentary on the New Testament*, describes what being born again means in a very powerful way. This comes from his reflections in the Gospel of John Chapter 3:

"1. What it is that is required: to be born again; that is, First, We must live a new life. Birth is the beginning of life; to be born again is to begin anew, as those that have hitherto lived either much amiss or to little purpose. We must not think to patch up the old building, but begin from the foundation. Secondly, We must have a new nature, new principles, new affections, new aims. We must be born anōthen, which signifies both denuo— again, and desuper—from above. 1. We must be born anew; so the word is taken, our first birth we are corrupt, shapen in sin and iniquity; we must therefore undergo a second birth; our souls must be fashioned and enlivened anew. 2. We must be born from above, so the word is used by the evangelist (ch. 3:31) and I take this to be especially intended here, not excluding the other; for to be born from above supposes being born again. But this new birth has its rise from heaven (ch. 1:13) and its tendency to heaven: it is to be born to a divine and heavenly life, a life of communion with God and the upper world, and, in order to this, it is to partake of a divine nature and bear the image of the heavenly."

OBSTACLES TO PUTTING ON THE NEW SELF

Fear of the Holy Spirit
To put on the new self, we need to be dependent on and living in the Holy Spirit. There are many Christians who are unsure and somewhat fearful of the Holy Spirit. This fear may be because they are afraid of becoming too emotional when they depend on the Holy Spirit. It may simply be fear of the concept of a "spirit" which often has negative connotations as seen in the evil realm of the spiritual world.

Lack of Self-Forgiveness
Many Christians put themselves down for past sins and are carrying a lot of guilt. They may feel forgiven by Jesus, but they have not forgiven themselves and do not feel complete in Jesus. However, their sins have been forgiven as far as the east is from the west (Psalm 103:12). This lack of self-forgiveness creates insecurity and takes away the ability to live in the new self. We need to keep short accounts of our sins and immediately confess them to Jesus. He will forgive us and then we can forgive ourselves.

If there are major sins in our lives, they will take longer to work through. Not all sin affects us in the same spiritual, mental and emotional ways, and the peace of forgiveness may not be immediately felt. Whether it is a major or minor sin, the process of self-forgiveness involves varying degrees of emotional pain. When we sin, we are harming our Savior, ourselves and maybe others.

Once forgiveness has been received, some Christians relive the specifics of their sins, which can perpetuate feelings of guilt. When we sin we need to be specific in our confession, but once we have forgiveness, we need to make it less specific and label it simply as a negative event. Satan is into the specifics of sins because he is the accuser of the brethren (Revelation 12:10), and he has it down to a detailed science. Our Lord Jesus specifically wants us to only feel the peace of forgiveness.

Life Experiences

Some people assume when they become Christian, the negative issues from their past will instantly be resolved. In reality, the only way to put emotional negativity behind us is to take ownership of the truth and allow the truth to be within us. Dealing with our backgrounds and how they negatively affect our present lives releases burdens that keep us from the freshness found in the new self.

Christians Living a Double Life

Many Christians live a double life, which prevents them from living in the new self. They may attend church and have an air of spirituality, but their personal lives are actually unnatural combinations of the old self with the new self. We cannot truly live in the old and new self: it has to be one or the other. When we live in the new self we are free, but not free to sin. We are free from condemnation (Romans 8:1), free to love the Godhead, free to love ourselves and free to love others.

A Dependency on Others
When we look to people and are unto them instead of the Lord Jesus, we give them control of our lives instead of giving that power to the Holy Spirit.

One's Relationship with Their Parents
Negativity or a lack of closeness with one or both parents can be an obstacle to putting on the new self. This can involve the past parent/child relationship or can involve the present-day adult relationship. Unresolved issues with one's parents can cause enormous emotional turmoil.

Recognizing the Individuality
As Christians, we balance relationships with God and our personal/emotional life. The unique juxtaposition allows us, as individuals to be unified with the Father, Son, and Holy Spirit, without losing our unique identity. This is what we see in the Godhead bodily; they are unified, but have their own separate, unique individual identities as persons.

Self-rejection

Most Christians reject themselves and the positive they bring to the world. They are so afraid of being prideful or being seen as overconfident that they have developed a pattern of rejecting themselves. It is good to be proud of who we are in the Lord Jesus Christ when we're living a quality Christian life, because we are complete in Him. Romans 14:22 says, *"Hast thou faith? Have it to thyself before God. Happy is he that condemneth not himself in that thing which he alloweth."* Accepting the good in ourselves allows us to put on the new self.

Chapter 5

Putting on the New Self

PUTTING OFF / PUTTING ON

In Ephesians 4:22–24, the Apostle Paul says, *"That ye put off concerning the former conversation the old man, which is corrupt according to the deceitful lusts; And be renewed in the spirit of your mind; And that ye put on the new man, which after God is created in righteousness and true holiness."*

Paul is saying there is a deliberate action - rejection - that takes place when moving from the old self ("former conversation") to the new self ("the new man"). When rejecting the old self and accepting the new self there is no need to dwell on the old self; the action of putting off and putting on is complete. However, many Christians focus energy on the old self by mentally condemning or hating the old behavior and making sure (being on the alert) it doesn't overwhelm as it once did. Simply put, we laboriously attempt to do the work that only the Godhead can do.

What we have inside of us as Christians is immeasurable. We have the God of the universe in three persons inside of us. Our inadvertent dwelling on the old self does not trust Jesus, God the Father, and the Holy Spirit to be our God. Are they not powerful enough, holy enough and loving enough to protect us from this old self? In a numbers game, it is four to one against the old self. Satan and the world are outside of us. First John 4:4 says *"Ye are of God, little children, and have overcome them: because greater is he that is in you, than he that is in the world."* There is no need for the battle between the new self and the old self, just as there is no need for a battle between Satan and us. We need to allow the Lord Jesus to focus on this old self and destroy it. He knows what the flesh is all about, because He was not just fully God but fully man. He is at the ready to forgive us when we sin, but we need to accept His forgiveness and allow Him to continue the battle as we focus on Him and our life.

When we focus on the old self we focus way too much on ourselves. It is not the focus of selfishness or self-centeredness, but a focus of self-involvement. When we focus on the old self we are constantly involved with wondering what our thoughts mean, and are constantly worried about the power of the old self. This puts us on high alert and creates enormous amounts of anxiety and a lack of peace, which put us in bondage to fear.

FAITH, LOVE AND PRINCIPLES

"As ye have therefore received Christ Jesus the Lord, so walk ye in him:" In Colossians 2:6 the Apostle Paul says we need to live our Christian lives in faith, because that's how we initially received Jesus as Lord

and Savior. We are given spiritual new life, power and energy that lead to a walk (dependency) with the Holy Spirit (Second Corinthians 5:5–7). Dr. Charles Caldwell Ryrie discusses this in his book *The Holy Spirit*:

"Finally, the Spirit-filled life is a dependent life. "But I say, walk by the Spirit, and you will not carry out the desire of the flesh" (Galatians 5:16) . . .

. . . In this verse in Galatians the Christian is reminded that in order to walk and make progress in the Christian life, he must walk by faith, which means to live in dependence on the Holy Spirit . . ."

However, faith alone is a sounding brass. God the Father wants us to have love first and then faith coming by that love second (not faith by itself). It's not, "I am a man of faith," but "I am a man of faith by love." A faith that emerges out of love is the proper faith for the Christian life.

When we are living in this way we will bear the fruit of the Holy Spirit for all to see, including ourselves. We won't have to worry if we're getting it right or wrong. Paul's letter to the Galatians reminded them of this necessary faith and love combination. He says in Galatians 5:5–6, *"For we through the Spirit wait for the hope of righteousness by faith. For in Jesus Christ neither circumcision availeth any thing, nor uncircumcision; but faith which worketh by love."*

The Galatians had become fixated on the bondage of works and legalism, and had lost their first love relationship. They were using the principle of right and wrong with condemnation instead of using faith and love to bring freedom without condemnation. The first establishment for our salvation was not our faith (belief), but God's love. The Father could have condemned us by focusing exclusively on principles. Instead he chose love and that love for us opened the door to belief in salvation. It is that gift that overcomes condemnation found in principles that come without love. Jesus reveals in John 3:16-17, *"For God so loved the world, that he gave his only begotten Son, that whosoever believeth in him should not perish, but have everlasting life. For God sent not his Son into the world to condemn the world; but that the world through him might be saved."*

Like the Galatians, much of today's evangelical Christianity in America has also left its first love. In the 1970s there was much discussion and teaching about developing a close, loving relationship with Jesus as a vital focus to one's Christian life. It was a wonderful time not only to hear how much God loves us, but to also experience it with Jesus. Since then, the focus overwhelmingly has become the development of principles in one's life.

When we focus on principles over a relationship to the Godhead, it allows principles to be our God, and creates two negatively dynamic experiences. The first is a lifestyle of works, and the second is an emotional pattern of highly charged fear. Both create self-criticism and/or self-hatred because of the focus to be perfect or the extreme need to "get it just right." The ultimate Biblical verse about principle is the "The Great Commandment." A Pharisee lawyer was trying to force Jesus to declare that principles were the most important aspect of living a moral life. The Pharisees and Sadducees had the commandments of right and wrong down to a science. They lacked love of God and others and in focusing on their principled process they became evil (Matthew 23:13–33). The good old legalists must have been aghast when they heard Jesus' response. *"But when the*

Pharisees had heard that he had put the Sadducees to silence, they were gathered together. Then one of them, which was a lawyer, asked him a question, tempting him, and saying, Master, which is the great commandment in the law? Jesus said unto him, Thou shalt love the Lord thy God with all thy heart, and with all thy soul, and with all thy mind. This is the first and great commandment. And the second is like unto it, Thou shalt love thy neighbour as thyself. On these two commandments hang all the law and the prophets." (Matthew 22:34–40)

The Pharisees and Sadducees had been putting these principled commandments on people with terrible guilt, shame and brutal burden. The cure for fear escaped them. John said in 1 John 4:18 that, *"There is no fear in love; but perfect love casteth out fear: because fear hath torment. He that feareth is not made perfect in love."* Whether modern Christian leaders lay serious amounts of guilt and shame is not a major point (although many are putting onto others the fear of what God will do to them if they break His commandments). Just the mere emphasis of principles over a loving relationship will create serious anxiety and fear every time. It is a fear that comes from having to perform perfectly with rights and wrongs and the fear of letting God down. As John expressed in 1 John 4:18, if there is anything we are trying to perfect we need to try to perfect love (not principle).

Jesus doesn't say that principles, commandments and the law are not vitally important. He says there are things that must have greater emphasis. Faith, hope, and love, and the greatest of these is love (First Corinthians 13:13). He stressed a loving relationship between God (all three persons), ourselves and others. What He also presented was the sequence of how this happens: First loving God the Father, God the Son and God the Holy Spirit; then we are able to love who we are; and finally we are able to love others because we first loved God and ourselves. We have a lot of love to give when we have experienced, and possessed love ourselves. It's like money — if we have a lot of money we can give a lot of money away. If we don't have any money we don't have any money to give away. The amount of water that flows through a creek is dependent on its source.

PRINCIPLES AND FAMILIES

The problem of principles over loving relationships is prevalent in modern-day Christian families. Many Christian parents put a priority on principles over relationships with their children. In doing so, they do not have a loving relationship with their children, become very authoritarian with discipline and create an enormous amount of anxiety and fear. A parent's principles in discipline need to come out of a loving relationship. There are more than a few areas of right and wrong where children need to feel their parents give them freedom without putting them under a pile of punishment.

Chapter 6

A Loving Relationship with God the Father, God the Son, God the Holy Spirit, Ourselves and Others

Our love for God the Father, God the Son and God the Holy Spirit should be in equal measure for each Person. Many Christians are confused about the Holy Spirit in part because the Lord Jesus is heavily positioned in the foreground of our lives. This closeness with Jesus represents the most important area of emphasis in our Christian lives, but we still need to be filled with love equally for each in the Godhead. We identify overwhelmingly with Jesus, then with the Father and finally with the Holy Spirit. Apostle Paul says the new self is in the Lord Jesus. Ephesians 2:10 says, *"For we are his workmanship, created in Christ Jesus unto good works, which God hath before ordained that we should walk in them."*

In his book, *Matthew Henry's Commentary On The New Testament*, Matthew Henry gives great insight on this verse from Second Peter 1:3: *"According as his divine power hath given unto us all things that pertain unto life and godliness, through the knowledge of him that hath called us to glory and virtue:"*

> "Observe, (1.) The fountain of all spiritual blessings is the divine power of Jesus Christ, who could not discharge all the office of Mediator, unless he was God as well as man. (2.) All things that have any relation to, and influence upon, the true spiritual life, the life and power of godliness, are from Jesus Christ; in him all fullness dwells, and it is from him that we receive, and grace for grace . . ."

LOVING YOURSELF

THE COMMANDMENT TO LOVE OURSELVES

In addition to learning to love and understand the Holy Spirit, learning to love and understand ourselves is the hardest area of love to implement. It is also an essential love that builds our Christian faith. There are still some Christians who do not believe in loving oneself even though it is clearly in the Word of God.

Matthew 22:37–39 says, *"Jesus said unto him, Thou shalt love the Lord thy God with all thy heart, and with all thy soul, and with all thy mind. This is the first and great commandment. And the second is like unto it, Thou shalt love thy neighbour as thyself."*

We can love ourselves because we are imitators of God and Jesus, who have always loved us. We need to learn to love ourselves the way that they love us. Much of our lives are lived on our own, even if we are around others. Self-love overcomes the need to become co-dependent on others.

Self-love occurs after we have surrendered everything to the Lord. After the surrender, it is our responsibility to use our God-given life for His glory. This surrender and love of self allows a deeper love for the Godhead and others. Those who do not believe in loving themselves focus on the old self, which admittedly does not deserve to be loved. We need to reconcile ourselves dead to sin, but alive through Jesus (Romans 6:11). When we are alive in this new life we can love our new self.

THE NEGATIVE PREOCCUPATION WITH INTROSPECTION

One of the great roadblocks for Christians is a preoccupation with introspection. Christians who constantly introspect are constantly evaluating and overanalyzing their thoughts, feelings and even their physiology. This over-inspection is not due to selfishness or self-centeredness, but self-involvement, analyzing, scrutinizing and searching. They are searching to make sure that they are spiritual enough, and therefore a good Christian. They do not allow the Lord Jesus to do the searching while they do the living. If there's a problem or sin in our life He will let us know about it. Jesus is focused perfectly and constantly on us at all times to help make us better believers so that we don't have to attempt to play God. He is God and we need to allow Him to be. In Him pertaineth all things that are necessary to life and godliness (Second Peter 1:3). We are complete in Him, and in Him we have all we need.

Many Christians are overly concerned about almost every negative thought. This habit creates an enormous amount of brain tiredness. People are mentally tired from working so hard to control or figure out what every thought means. We can try to figure out if the thought is from others, from Satan or from ourselves. Or we can simply give the thought to the Lord so we can avoid all of the energy it would take to figure it out. Negative thinking usually ends up in self-judgment not self-love, because the negativity piles up and we fear the worst about ourselves. One will experience great stress and imbalance instead of experiencing the freedom that is found in faith as a result of love. The stress makes it difficult to be renewed so that the new self can flourish (Ephesians 4:22–24). The mind is renewed and refreshed not by mental busywork and bondage, but by the freedom of a renewed and restored mind that is easier to manage. A tired mind is much more prone to negative thinking. Proverbs 16:3 has a wonderful solution for the fear and mistrust of the mind: *"Commit thy works unto the LORD, and thy thoughts shall be established."* When we live out our days unto the Lord He will establish our thoughts, and we will not have to worry about them.

A powerful prayer to help to overcome extreme self-introspection is: "Lord Jesus, free me from myself." Perfect love casts out fear (1 John 4:18), and this perfect love includes avoiding over-analysis, criticism and self-judgment. We can love ourselves by not living in fear, but by "moving out" and believing we can be free from bondage.

Another way to love ourselves so that we don't get caught up in introspection is to forget prior introspection and minimize dwelling too much on the future. Unless facing one's background or experiences is necessary for moving forward in a healthy way, forgetting the past is usually the right course. The Apostle Paul says in Philippians 3:13, *"Brethren, I count not myself to have apprehended: but this one thing I do, forgetting those things which are behind, and reaching forth unto those things which are before,"* Paul is saying we need to live with urgency in what is before us now. If we dwell too much on the past, we can't live in the now, and the now is where the ultimate and abundant Christian life can be experienced. We love ourselves in our new self when we "Work hard and play hard." Movement allows us to focus better on the present than the past or the future. Being still often allows the mind to wander too much. There is time for rest and relaxation, but much of our time needs to be spent in movement.

It is important to have a vision, a dream or a plan for our lives. However, a preoccupation in wanting to be the "better me" in the future creates a lot of pressure. Our Christian life is one of process and development, and we need to accept where we are and who we are today. Avoiding an over-emphasis on the future lets us enjoy and love ourselves today. A simple experiment to avoid introspection can prove the point. If an individual gets involved with something positive without immediately reflecting on how he feels about it, he will almost always experience a much better sense of self. This is because the focus is not on what's in the mind, but what is actually happening.

PRAYING TOO MUCH

Another reason many Christians have difficulty loving themselves is that they are praying all the time rather than focusing on tasks at hand and resting their minds. It is definitely possible to pray too much. Many take the verse First Thessalonians 5:17 which says "Pray without ceasing" out of context and are tiring their minds by praying constantly. The Wycliffe Bible Commentary gives very good insight on this verse: "17. Prayer is attitude as well as activity. The attitude of devotion to God can be without ceasing (cf. note on 1:3), if the activity cannot. Paul illustrates his own command, for his letters are scented with the fragrance of prayer." When we try to pray all the time in an active way we are "Becoming so heavenly minded that we are no earthly good." A tired mind is not a mind that is free and able to care for oneself.

A LOT OF EXPECTATION

It is difficult to love oneself when one is expecting too much. A good quote that can help alleviate the pressure is "You can't do any more than you can do." Most Christians put enormous expectations on themselves to do beyond what even God wants them to do. This pressure creates a lot of anxiety and negative emotions. We don't have to do anything that we don't want to do. God the Father doesn't want us chained to stress from driving ourselves too hard. He wants us to do His will with a free and happy heart.

TAKING CARE OF THE PHYSICAL

Perhaps the most important thing we can do to love ourselves is to take care of ourselves physically. If we don't take care of ourselves physically, we cannot carry out what we want and need to do. Many people are realizing the benefits of healthy eating, exercise and moderate amounts of sunlight. Another positive change people are making is adding supplements to their diets. An outstanding reference on supplements is leading nutrition journalist Bill Sardi, who wrote *The New Truth About Vitamins & Minerals*.

Some are going through very difficult emotional and mental struggles but are misdiagnosing those struggles as strictly emotional issues. In his book, *Control of the Circulation*, Frederick Erdman says mental and emotional difficulty is often due to a lack of proper blood circulation. Poor circulation can cause serious brain fog and mental phobias, which can create serious anxiety or fear. One can try to face this with a counselor, but the real cause and solution lies in the physical realm to bring back the proper blood flow. Two great techniques to help circulation are moderate exercise and relaxation. Severe circulation issues should be addressed with a physician.

Self-massage techniques dealing with trigger point therapy are outlined in *The Trigger Point Therapy Workbook: Second Edition*, by Clair Davies with Amber Davies. These techniques produce tremendous results in reducing chronic fatigue, pain and recurrence of De Quervain's Tenosynovitis.

We Love Ourselves by Learning to Control Our Mind

It is alarming to see Christians involved in the world of imagination and fantasy. Some of the fantasy world may be Christian in nature, but a lot of it is not. It can be very dangerous to imagine and fantasize to the great degree that many of our young people do.

Teaching our children to be heavily involved in imagination and fantasy must be paired (at least) equally with giving those imaginations and fantasies to the Lord Jesus in obedience (Second Corinthians 10:5). An imaginative mind burns with creativity. Adding in a fantastical element creates a more dynamic mind, but can also lead to sleeplessness, anxiety and a need to maintain the excitement and energy associated with it.

Young or adolescent girls are going to be affected much more than boys in the arena of the imaginative. This is because girls typically feel more emotions than boys, and as a consequence are going to be affected more negatively.

We Love Ourselves by Controlling Our Emotions

The way we control our emotions is to embrace and express them. This is true for positive and negative emotions. Positive emotions must be felt and expressed so that they can be released, and free us up for the next positive feelings. Negative emotions must be released because they do the most damage. The inability to release emotions will cause serious emotional and mental problems that will begin to break us down.

Adults really need to live with emotions the way most children live. Watch a child playing. They fall and start to cry, but their hurt and fear is short-lived. When they are able to feel and release the hurt and fear, they go back to playing with smiles and joy. An outstanding book is Hudson Taylor's *Spiritual Secret*, which reveals the two elements of this secret. Taylor enjoyed a little harmonium for refreshment, playing and singing favorite hymns. However, he always went back to Jesus. "I am resting, resting, in the joy of what Thou art; I am finding out the greatness of Thy loving heart." Day and night, this was his other secret: "just to roll the burden on the Lord . . ." He had learned that only one life was possible; the blessed life of resting and rejoicing in the Lord under all circumstances, while He dealt with the difficulties, inward and outward, great and small.

LOVING OTHERS

When we love God the Father, God the Son, God the Holy Spirit, and ourselves we are in a position to love others in a very significant way. If the first two areas of love are shortchanged than we do not have the foundation to love others in any large part. These prior loving relationships must develop in order for us to be able to develop loving relationships with others.

The biggest problem preventing Christians from truly loving others is dependency. It is easy to become dependent on others, because they literally are second in line to become Godlike to us if we do not allow the one and true God to be Himself in a relational loving way. If we do not have God then we will have people. There is an over-emphasis of fellowship with others in many parts of America; from public school systems to evangelical Christianity. In many of those areas, a relationship with God has been by relationships only with people.

Another issue is the attempt to control others, whether in trying to love or in receiving love. Rather than letting the person be who they are, someone tries to turn them into what he or she wants them to be. This creates a serious problem in a relationship that is seeking love as its foundation. Love does not control. People who are being controlled do not feel loved, but rejected for being themselves. In loving others, we need to "take them where they are," not move them to where we want them to be.

Many Christians expect way too much from other Christians. They often expect even more than what God expects, putting way too much pressure on the person loving or being loved. Many times the expectations are much less for themselves personally, than what they expect from others. A person needs to love unconditionally and not expect any gratefulness or appreciation. A person receiving love needs to allow the other person to love them in their own special way even if it is different from what they expect or want.

WE LOVE OURSELVES AND LIVE IN THE NEW SELF BY GROWING IN OUR SELF-ASSURANCE (CONFIDENCE)

Self-assurance Enhancement Traits

There are certain elements of an individual's self-confidence that can be implemented and grow. Self-confidence gives us a great sense of well being and strength. When we grow and develop our self-confidence we are greatly loving ourselves and living powerfully in our new self. Character is closely linked to one's self-confidence, because many of the same elements of self-confidence can be found in individual character. Consequently as we grow in our human character we grow in our self-confidence and vice versa. Here are some traits of self-assurance:

Self-expression: This can take the form of verbal communication, athletic activity or artistic expression. It is important to share our individual expression to others so it is not trapped inside. When who we are remains locked up inside, it creates serious insecurity and anxiety. There are more forms of expression than just verbal communication, which is the most important for most individuals, but is not the only way to share our emotions.

Risk-taking: Many people have trouble taking risks and stay in the same-old difficult circumstances or relationships. When we face the fear of taking a risk by carefully considering and then executing that change, we can get out of difficult experiences and develop our inner strength.

Honesty: We love ourselves enormously when we are honest and open with ourselves and with others. The courage to be truthful (as well as the truth itself) sets us free.

Courage: Facing difficult experiences with courage helps develop tremendous strength and self-assurance.

Self-awareness and acceptance: Most people do not know themselves as well as they think they do. Self-awareness helps discover likes and dislikes, positives and negatives, personality type, and so on. When we figure out who we are, it frees us up to accept who we are and not try to be someone else. When we live in our new self we are much more prone to accept who we are and avoid self-rejection. If we accept the Lord Jesus' love and encouragement, then we can accept the person we are. If we avoid a pattern of sin, we will more easily love and accept ourselves.

Decisiveness: Decisiveness comes from a sense of confidence instead of a fear of failure. Decisiveness is a very important component of self-confidence, because the ability to make clear and timely decisions brings about a sense of inner freedom.

Self-encouragement: Many times we look to others to give us desperately needed encouragement. This is a problem because others are going through difficult times themselves, and they're not in a position to give much encouragement. The best way to develop a consistent pattern of encouragement in our lives is to encourage ourselves. This encouragement is a great positive approach against the negative build-up of life.

Self-assurance (confidence): If someone had an emotional closeness with their same-sex parent, then he or she will have a natural tendency to feel self-confident, even in difficult or highly negative situations. If someone did not have this emotional closeness then he needs to identify with Jesus. When we identify with Him, we receive the blessing of a new self-confidence found in Him and ourselves. The solution to individual insecurity is most powerfully realized in Jesus Christ.

Self-trust: When we trust ourselves we feel less insecure and more at peace. A lack of self-trust creates enormous anxiety and weakness. Staying active and busy creates opportunities for building day and/or life plans and self-trust.

Self-responsibility: It seems very few people are taking advantage of this self-confidence trait and the strength that goes with it. When we are responsible for ourselves, we become less dependent on others. When we're less dependent on others, we will experience a sense of strength that comes along with living our lives as true individuals.

Self-commitment: This has to do with the level of urgency and persistence that an individual has in loving themselves and in developing their new self and self-assurance. Most things in life that are important take commitment, time and perseverance. Learning to love oneself is no exception.

GROWING IN OUR INDIVIDUAL CHRISTIAN CHARACTER

The Apostle Paul in Galatians 5:22–23 wrote, *"But the fruit of the Spirit is love, joy, peace, longsuffering, gentleness, goodness, faith, Meekness, temperance: against such there is no law."*

It is fascinating that this first verse starts with the greatest character of all – love - and ends with a declaration against the dos and don'ts of the system of law. It highlights the emphasis of love (which is not a system, but founded in a relationship) over principle. The Father wants us to do our part and the Holy Spirit will do His larger part.

The greatest character of all is love, and that includes loving ourselves. When we make the decision to love ourselves and implement that love, we are developing the highest form of character. We should have a positive affection of fondness for ourselves and see ourselves as the best of friends, not the worst of enemies. Here are some of the positive character attributes:

Joy: When we are joyful with ourselves we will have more energy, happiness, smiles, a feeling of positive abundance, contentment and the ability to enjoy fun if we so choose to have some. Speaking of the word fun, Howard Blandau, psychologist and spiritual advisor, used to tell a humorous story about his time working with juvenile delinquents in Iowa. He would read those kids the riot act and say that if they had fun they were going to have a funeral. His punch line was something to the effect of, "Don't you understand that the first three letters in funeral are F-U-N, and if you go out and have fun you're going to have a funeral!" The juveniles' ideas of fun often included intoxication, drugs, stealing and other misdemeanors. In hindsight, he knew he had made a mistake with his fun/funeral rant, but that his intentions were good. As the years passed Howard realized that fun was an essential part to a joyous Christian life. His fun with the word "fun" had taken on a different tone. He started asking his clients if they had fun, and many times they would respond by just saying "fun?" with a question mark in their tone of voice. Howard would then say, "Yeah, fun- "F-U-N." He then would say something lovingly to the effect of, "If you don't have fun you're going to have a funeral. The first three letters in the word funeral are "F-U-N." The overwhelming majority of mid-life and older Christians have put joy and fun on the backburner so often that when they could have joy they have a difficult time owning and experiencing it. They need to allow themselves the true joy of energized happiness and cheerfulness that brings about a renewed sense of strength in their lives at any age. This kind of approach to life allows the happenings of life to be meaningful and purposeful. The joy of the Lord is our strength, but so is our own personal joy and the joy from the Holy Spirit.

Peace: We are at greatest peace and calm when we are living in the new self and emphasizing our Christian faith founded in love. When we do this, we can avoid self-hatred, self-judgment and self-rejection, which cause so much of our unrest.

Long-suffering: Suffering is the hardest fruit of the Spirit to swallow. No one enjoys suffering, yet we come upon a fascinating thing that occurs when we suffer; we have the consolation of the Lord Jesus Christ. In Second Corinthians 1:5 it says, *"For as the sufferings of Christ abound in us, so our consolation also aboundeth by Christ."*

Consolation here means it is a union of our sufferings and the sufferings of Jesus. When we identify in the Lord Jesus, we identify and experience the kinds of things He suffered while He was on this earth. He was despised and rejected of men and if we live a quality Christian life, we will have to endure this suffering ourselves. We literally become much closer to Jesus when we suffer with issues regarding ourselves and others. We become closer to Him because He comforts us, understands our hurts and encourages us, in the midst of great difficulty, to move on. He is there in a unified way in our darkest hour and He will never leave us. His intimacy and incredible perfect love are a result of developing the character of long-suffering in our lives.

Gentleness: Many Christians are much too critical of themselves. When we are self-critical, we will not be stable, gentle, kind, mild and useful. A house divided with extreme criticism is destroyed, because it creates a great amount of hurt and fear.

Goodness: When we are loving ourselves in a positive way, we are being pleasant, kind, morally sound, positive, non-critical, self-accepting, character building and helpful to ourselves.

Faith: Our faith born by love is developed with a belief in the Father, the Son and Holy Spirit. We then need to have a growing faith in who we are as born-again believers with our new self, and how we can become wonderful Christian people. When we lose faith in ourselves, we become insecure and lack confidence. God the Father wants us to be strong so we can deal with the many difficulties that this life brings.

Meekness: "Gentle, mild, humble and meek," is how the *Strong's Talking Greek & Hebrew Dictionary* describes meekness. When we love ourselves with meekness we are not quick to judge ourselves, but are at a peace when we approach ourselves. Meekness is not "humble pie," which is a false sense of humility. True humility is the absence of haughtiness and high-mindedness, which is steeped in arrogance. This does not mean we cannot have tremendous confidence in our new self. The Apostle Paul was extremely confident in who he was a Christian, and yet he came on very strong (not arrogant) at times to others. Unfortunately, many in the faith believe that the Apostle Paul was arrogant, giving the negative label to what was actually tremendous inner strength and confidence found in Jesus and himself. Meekness is not weakness.

Temperance (Self-control): Self-control focuses on our Christian faith (especially the Lord Jesus), and the positive things in our lives. It also includes the control of our bodies, spirit, will and mind. This is to be done not in authoritarian domination, but in a gentle or expectant urgency that will help us experience a more positive existence. If our spirit is down and depressed, and we know there's nothing negative that is causing it, we need to enjoy life more. If the mind is negative or sinful and our will is weak, we need to take control by redirecting thoughts to give us a more positive and energized mind.

WE LOVE OURSELVES BY CONTROLLING THE SPIRITUAL AREA OF OUR LIVES

Spirituality is the most important area of our lives. It is the most dynamic, energizing and deepest part of our individual beings. It is a blast furnace that must be dealt with. If we do not take control and mature in our Christian spirituality, we will be open to the control of non-Christian influences. We become prey to the whims of Satan when we are not increasing our faith founded by a loving relationship with God the Father, God the Son, and God the Holy Spirit. The simple faith relationship approach depends on the Holy Spirit, being relationally/socially close to the Lord Jesus, and glorifying and honoring the Father. If we do these things effectively we will control our spirituality and live in our new self.

Bibliography

1918. Database WORDsearch Corp., 2008.

Control Of The Circulation: By Physical Methods. Erdman, Frederick. Copyright ©, 1956, by Frederick Erdmann. Second Edition. Published by Frederick Erdman Association, 2050 West Chester Pike Havertown, PA 19083.

He That Is Spiritual. Chafer, Lewis Sperry. Copyright © 1918 by Lewis Sperry Chafer. Revised Edition, Copyright 1967 by Zondervan. Zondervan, Grand Rapids, Michigan 49530 USA.

Holy Bible. King James Version. Database WORDsearch Corp., 2007.

Holy Spirit, The. Ryrie, Charles Caldwell. 1965, 1997 Database WORDsearch Corp., 2006.

Hudson Taylor's Spiritual Secret. Taylor, Dr. and Mrs. Howard. Copyright © 1989 by The Moody Bible Institute of Chicago. Moody Press, Chicago.

Matthew Henry's Commentary On The New Testament. Parson's Church Group, a division of Findex. Com, Inc. Omaha, Nebraska. Quick Verse.com. Copyrights—*Matthew Henry's Commentary On The New Testament* Electronic Edition STEP Files Copyright © 2000, Findex.Com. All rights reserved.

New Unger's Bible Dictionary, The. Unger, Merrill F. Chicago, Illinois: Moody Press of Chicago, 1988. Database WORDsearch Corp., 2003.

Ryrie Study Notes. Ryrie, Charles Caldwell. Chicago: The Moody Bible Institute of Chicago, 1986, 1995. Database WORDsearch Corp., 2004.

Strong's Concordance. Strong, James. Text and Database WORDsearch Corp., 2007.

Strong's Talking Greek and Hebrew Dictionary. Strong, James. Text and Database WORDsearch Corp., 2007.

The New Truth About Vitamins & Minerals. Sardi, Bill. © Copyright Bill Sardi 2003. www.askbillsardi.com. Published by Here & Now Books, 457 West Allen Avenue # 117 San Dimas, CA 91773. First Edition Printing: April 2003, Second Edition Printing: May 2004.

The Ryrie KJV Study Bible. Ryrie, Charles Caldwell. Copyright © 1986, 1994 by The Moody Bible Institute of Chicago. Moody Publishers, Chicago.

The Trigger Point Therapy Workbook, Second Edition. Your Self-Treatment Guide For Pain Relief. Davies, Clair NCTMB with Amber Davies, NCTMB. Copyright © 2004 by Clair Davies. New Harbinger Publications, Inc. 5674 Shattuck Avenue, Oakland, CA 94609.

Wycliffe Bible Commentary, The. Pfeiffer, Charles F. and Harrison, Everett F. Chicago: The Moody Bible Institute of Chicago, 1962, 1990. Database WORDsearch Corp, 2008.

Legal Statements/ Disclaimer

1. Howard Blandau authorized me to receive and take ownership of all benefits (including financial) that result from the use of his insights, thoughts, ideas, etc. This includes this book entitled *LifeSights: Book Two — Old Self/New Self*, or any other written material, presented material, or production of any sort, which are the individual, combined and/or unified insights, thoughts or ideas, etc. of Howard Blandau and/or T. George Homsher.

2. A number of words, headings or statements that are made in this book, and the books in the *LifeSights* series, are those that I remember coming from Howard Blandau. I am unable to distinguish which words, headings or statements are his, and which words, headings or statements came from another source. If any stated quotes, concepts or thoughts are originally from someone else, the author greatly apologizes. Evidence of this would be greatly appreciated, and upon analysis if a mistake has been made, I will either identify the author of the stated quote, concept or thought and/or will reword them in a later edition of the book.

3. This book in no way is intended to be used to diagnose, treat, or cure any specific individual problem(s). Individuals are highly recommended to see a qualified helping professional, pastor, medical doctor or other professional to help diagnose, treat, and/or cure their specified problem(s).

www.ingramcontent.com/pod-product-compliance
Lightning Source LLC
Chambersburg PA
CBHW022130280326
41933CB00007B/631